PICNIC WITH SEA FOG AND ELEPHANTS

Sue MacIntyre

PICNIC WITH SEA FOG AND ELEPHANTS

The Many Press
London

Published by The Many Press, 15 Norcott Road, London N16 7BJ
ISBN 0 907326 37 4
Copyright © Sue MacIntyre London 2003
Printed by the Arc and Throstle Press, Todmorden

Cover design by Amanda Welch

Acknowledgement
'Christmas Present for My Mother' appeared in the anthology *Parents*,
edited by Myra Schneider and Dilys Wood (Enitharmon).

CONTENTS

Waking Elegy   7
Unpeopled Morning   8
Visitation   9
Piero   10
Ambushed by Notes   11
Christmas Present for My Mother   12
Dress with Vines   13
Sunflower Harvest   15
Remembering Elephants   16
Setting Sail   17
Shutters   18
Normandy, September 2001   19
'Sun in an Empty Room' by Edward Hopper   20
Painted Wooden Boat, Egyptian   21
Trampled Mint   22
Picnic with Sea Fog and Elephants   24

Waking Elegy

A hand is sliding the dolls forward slowly
out of sleep. They begin to take their places on the window sill.
The pawns are moved up into the sunrise
and slowly I remember there are gaps on the chess table
that can't be filled, moves that can never be made again.

Opening myself to sounds of the ivy garden where
the rustle of squirrels muffles the terracotta armies in the earth
and distant birds sing of god's election plan
and the lost embroidered routes, I try

to hold back a while longer, to stay hidden
and not yet see the shapes of old cacti on the window sill,
not yet move into the world of 'and then'
where the boy at the desk is still doing his word puzzle,
making loops around the letters word by word,
delay climbing the hard shoulder and finding that
when I open my eyes
a revenant is only a space-between.

Unpeopled Morning

The trees suck me out of bed at five o'clock in the morning,
staring deep into the eyeless trees, their colourless velvet,
their gustiness speaking only tree.

I'm absent from the sky, the vibrating cool of deep blue
and monochrome of the hills,
the darkness of light before dawn.

The trees have taken over again, blotting us out,
and the rooster begins talking only rooster
through his unseen scrawny neck.

I can rest in these unpeopled spaces
which carry on without us,
our gestures, our interferences,

without our language lying on the land,
our little mixed reading,
our lists, our programmes,

and when early morning air creeps in
through a gap in the door,
how could I ever name it, its white scents?

Visitation

You are shy,
you are goatlike,
you come in early morning
unpeopledness,
light eyes curious,
head heavy with a budding horn.
Not a whiff of farmyard,
musky scent of whiteness,
nesting for a moment
near my pillow's whiteness,
bringing with you
a sense that sets dreams reeling,
that enlightenment and eternity
have white curly hair on their skins.
You trail the scent of countries
where people have never been.
You trot in to graze at my pillow
and leave a bag of milk by my head

Piero

It's going slowly: wings –
I've been thinking about the wings, this angel, these angels,
the blondness I've seen surprising in the street.
A sturdy boy, curly hair, so upright, his feet
planted. A procession – his eyes towards the fields.
He was right, but earthed.
The wings are like, I've found the colours, they are –
huge – rich crimson and green flowing down
but they're heavy. He's heavy.
How can they lift him? And the joining – feathers
growing out of this solidness? They look
folded away, unused.

Folded away . . . perhaps, yes, half-hidden,
the glimmering, hint of feathers
behind the shoulders, or not there at all.
I'll keep the boy,
the blond figures between . . . among . . . or
just standing, making music, legs thick stems,
like incidental crocuses in rough grass,
lit clearly, growing sturdily out of the mud
among the cigarette packets,
singly or in groups.

Ambushed by Notes
for my mother

Ambushed by notes –
those little notes he sends you,
your eldest grandson,
in the bottom of the sugar pot:
'white sugar is very bad for our bodies'
and on your shopping list:
'get organic',
and a daughter's message,
telling you to put a little oil
in the bath water
or the carer's, reminding you
what's there for lunch.
They skip the target,
they are vanishing faces,
the absent faces of care,
and your mind brushes past them
like knee-high wet grass
in the early morning.

Christmas Present for My Mother

Yes the bottle comes wrapped in bladderwrack,
in coils of slinky seaweed
and I'll pack it in a small wicker basket.
When you open it
sea smells will ooze out into your sitting room.
Quick we must take the bottle
and pour a streak of emerald green renewing oil
into your hot bath and hurry to help you,
your claw-like leg, slowly over the edge
and lower your stooping hesitant body
into the pungent greenish hot spring.
And we'll hover as you sigh
and lie back and say 'wonderful'
and your confusion, your grief, your wandering
will be steamed away
and your back will slowly become strong
and your voice as it used to be.
You'll push up out of the water forcefully
and call for your towel.
You won't be young again but
your strength will come back.
There'll be a whiff of you
in that old photograph on the seafront,
dressed in cascading streamers
of seaweed, laughing.

Dress with Vines

Remember how the colours went –
its huge vine-leaf wings and frog spawn eyes?

Bands of leaves red black red black,
bold orderly pairs of palms,

my mother's firm hands pressing me forward –
farther than I wanted to go into the world

where a solid young man waited.
She asked him whether he liked the dress,

its neck that's called heart-shaped, its full skirt.
'Yes,' he said, and thought. 'It's vinous.'

A big dipper ride – 'please open your eyes,' he begged.
The grape eyes were green with black circles and dots

staring out of a bed of white, as if she were
anxiously keeping its eyes on me.

Do you grow into what your clothes are saying?
Is that why choosing was anguish always?

I wasn't into the o'ervaulting, preening, tumbling out
into the world of fun she wanted for me.

Instead the dress belonged to
whoops – a *bal* in the village of Vouziers,

the champagne region, and the stranger who
asked me to dance – I stuck, and tripped up on his feet.

And it lasted like a flag, changed
to a skirt with a wide stiff waistband,

pushing me through my clumsy dancing years,
out of step, and she dancing beside me,

egging me on to roll back the carpet,
still beating through me, outstripping me.

Sunflower Harvest

This time I came to the valley in September.
It seemed filled with another crop – the crop
of the total eclipse of the moon,
the machines going heavily at night
under bright lights, harvesting tobacco
and sunflowers.

Before, the land was splashed with their yellow,
irradiating huge spaces, opening doors,
their erect heads anxiously turned
to stare at the sun.
I felt their loss –

now they are crumpled,
brown as bats,
crooked necks, small heads down,
the sun too dazzling
for their shadowed eyes.
I was chilled by what they had become –
such a spilling of self, such a shrinking –

remembering when you came to the door,
your face showing more than grief,
your world out of joint, as if
your sense of harvest was nothing more
than a spilled seedbasket.

Remembering Elephants

A summer trying to remember elephants, how they visited their dead,
their laying on of trunks, how they fondled the tusks of the dead,
staying on and on after the end.

In my mind still seeing them, oblivious in caravan, between the pillars
of King's Cross Station and the rushed concrete of other dead places
as I trail up and down England with my rucksack, my LL Bean bag,
like a student with a railcard and the mirage of family.

Those lost elephant ways of moving and thinking, how will I hold on to them?
The baby between the tree trunk legs, the moving forest
slowing down for him, the moving island coming back for him;

trampling past villagers' houses, stripping trees and tearing up bushes,
wickerwork of sun on their leathery backs, sun lighting up
the baby's forehead; and grandmother elephant sitting in the corner
of the kitchen knitting, her kind pig eyes and beauty lost.

Setting Sail
for Kate and Christophe

In spite of
the clear of everything in its place,
the hundred and sixty-four jobs still to be done
listed, jars labelled in black felt pen,
the new log opened,
the knot school,
the oar repaired again –

in spite of
the gasket at last
flown in from Athens,
the rope circles on deck
like giant bleached ammonites,
knotty insurance debates,
discussions striving
to be empty of everything
but careful planning –

in spite of
the Yamaha outboard motor at last
joined together in holy gasketry,
the tight white of the ship's world,
the tight visible cause and effect –

in the galley
a green swatch of dill, two halves of garlic clove
and a bottle top
make an accidental cartoon creature,
and brains exhausted with judgment
skip the weather forecast and are
flooded with let's go, let's go
off into the gale.

Shutters

The different forms of ajar and handed-down
degrees of darkness traditional
in these stone farmhouses, multiple permutations
for shutting out the light:

the casement's hinged and opens
inwards, the dark brown shutter hinged
on it. You can lock the shutter
to the casement with small coarse
blocks of wood, then hook the darkened window
half open and half shut – spillage of light
at top, at bottom, shield from heat or bats,

or in early morning unhook and swing
the whole thing open, both sides locked back
against the wall, rest on the sill, loll there, trying to
breathe white mist and the beginnings of sun,

or lock it all out, shut the heat and light away.
The lock's called *spagnoletta* –
a black rod the length of the window frame
and a handle. The frames groove tightly,
one turn and you're in the dark
black velvet on an iron bed,

lying remembering the Italian symphony
in a rush of mountain water, pinkish stones,
the quick evening closing of the sun, movement
of goats in the valley below, the only fear
that you can't still hold these things,
remember them, that you'll forget the clue
of lock, unlock, give up.

Normandy, September 2001

As if it's a row of picture dominoes –
this is the sliding rain, this
the placid house,
the trotting horse on yellow sand,
a baby's speckled sock,
a shining conker slitting its dingy case,
a willow tree, a flapping sole,
pram wheels, a rusty gun,
bright alphabet of white moon
in the garden,
green lanes with lost soldiers' names,
the withdrawn strip of sea
where words recede.

I match the pictures,
link their patterns on the table –
the toil of naming them.
Our holiday – bright, wordless world
where sentences slide down
into a ditch somewhere
back in the war of the hedgerows
with bodies of the dead.

'Sun in an Empty Room' by Edward Hopper

Light unfolds pleats of blond paper in your empty room.

Has your canvas been here the whole summer
waiting for this mellowing where brush-strokes fuzz bare walls,
looking for this space where sharp sunlight's shaded
by the wall's angle? What is your yellow now?

The sun didn't caress your people.
They're all dissolved now:
nighthawks, sea watchers,
cruel nudes in hotel rooms at 11 am,
transients, their luggage waiting,
flesh not at home in dark upholstery,
women standing on stripes of acid yellow
or staring at the white glare of high noon;
disjointed perched lives,
eyes never meeting
in the stuck fluorescent sun.
Your awkward brave comedians
have bowed out.

Now secret woods quicken outside your window.
Life seeps back more abundantly, differently.
White light turns the colour of sand.
Your empty room what are you after in it?
You said 'I'm after me.'

Sun sunlight sun in an empty room.

Painted Wooden Boat, Egyptian

Those birds, the just
touching the water blue wings
that know
the skimming way –

I'm following them – who
carefully hold the still
ant's egg, the seeds
in their little pods, trail,
flick their wings and then
point up again

their canopied heads –
easy, deft, touch of orange –
just thinking I'll eat these first,
under that branch, then forward
on the turquoise sheen.

I know it's death, carrying
my serious burden but don't
think it, and balance-magic,
the tree pose on water
will speed us to Abydos
undisturbed.

Trampled Mint

Horses' hooves
in the small hours of the morning
(gushing of water on the dusty road),
the blistered dark
cooled by the song,
ringing of hollow coconut shells.

In the small hours,
after the yelling rapacity of vespas,
the hot chafing of voices,
in a space left by all the trains
rattling across Europe
horses' hooves
startling as trampled mint.

1965

In my dream,
passing through the stale lecture hall,
nearing the end of my second English
first degree course,
I'm no farther forward
than the first time round.

My daughter's a student now,
pushing towards finals,
steady boyfriend –
seems like clear directedness
in a dusty red back-to-back
near Hyde Park in Leeds
and I am visiting her.

We heard the clop clop clop
of the rag-and-bone man's horse.
My dream pushes up the horses in Verona,
the poem I wrote then.

Coming up brown dream steps
to the brown college hall
I sense something small and green
on the carpeted floor –
sprigs of green mint pushing up –
more and more.

The line I didn't feel quite right in the old poem
lies in the dark brown soil of the dream carpet
and germinates there.

1990

Picnic with Sea Fog and Elephants
after a painting by Amanda Welch

They laid out their picnic on the lip
of the yellow sand, uneasy, not knowing
when the space would be engulfed again
by the trampling of the elephant cliffs,
the sea, the deadening wisps of sea fog.
There was no-one else there,
only a cowering house peering through
the elephant backs. They felt they would be
blotted out unless they ran away.
But the white cloth shimmered, near levitation.
It seemed it could float past the yellow emptiness
to a new element far away, a tongue of sea
shining, rolling, loosening limbs.
Before the fog came in there was a radiance
of empty yellow, the sea burnt blue.

In an aside in the back of the car,
half asleep, talking and dozing,
friends appearing and vanishing again like seals –
she said did you know George Love died in Brazil?
He would call us every now and then.
Death sneaked in like a wisp of sea fog.
We didn't notice at the time as we drove
up along the foggy coast. Sometimes
we would drive out of a fog bank.
For a moment there would be blazing
desert mountains, quick shock of the sea.
Jewel transparencies, promise, he never settled.